Listen to the newest episodes of our newest program *Heart of Business*, where we engage leaders who are masters of change and agents of transformation at http://bit.ly/2TN5HCR.

Transformational Leadership

8 Paradigm-Shifting Interviews from *Business Matters*

Thomas White
Founder Trnsform

Host and Executive Producer

ACTIONABLE JOURNAL

Email: info@trnsform.io
14606 NE 159th Street
Brush Prairie, WA 98606

Copyright © 2020, Trnsform Partners, LLC

All rights reserved. No part of this book shall be reproduced, stored in a retrieval system, or transmitted by any means other than through the AHAthat platform or with the same attribution shown in AHAthat without written permission from the publisher.

The author of each section owns the copyright of their own material.

Please go to
https://aha.pub/BusinessMatters
to read this AHAbook and to share the
individual AHAmessages that resonate with you.

Published by THiNKaha®
20660 Stevens Creek Blvd., Suite 210
Cupertino, CA 95014
https://thinkaha.com
E-mail: info@thinkaha.com

First Printing: April 2020
Hardcover ISBN: 978-1-61699-342-9   1-61699-342-1
Paperback ISBN: 978-1-61699-334-4   1-61699-334-0
eBook ISBN: 978-1-61699-335-1   1-61699-335-9
Place of Publication: Silicon Valley, California, USA
Paperback Library of Congress Number: 2019911622

Trademarks

All terms mentioned in this book that are known to be trademarks or service marks have been appropriately capitalized. Neither THiNKaha, nor any of its imprints, can attest to the accuracy of this information. Use of a term in this book should not be regarded as affecting the validity of any trademark or service mark.

Warning and Disclaimer

Every effort has been made to make this book as complete and as accurate as possible. The information provided is on an "as is" basis. The author(s), publisher, and their agents assume no responsibility for errors or omissions. Nor do they assume liability or responsibility to any person or entity with respect to any loss or damages arising from the use of information contained herein.

Acknowledgements

From 2008 through 2013, we produced *Business Matters*. Over that time, a number of very talented producers and contributors helped create the show. Each of these people made *Business Matters* better than I could have done alone.

The contributors to *Business Matters* were: Danielle Gunn, Andrew Scott Duncan, Alex Smith, Sherry White, Jonah Meadows, Christine Black, Raj'r Taim, Charlie Knower, Bill Motlong, Prudence Tippins, Kelly Mandarano, David Banner, and Robert Galinsky.

I'm grateful to our many guests. Your commitment to creating a public dialogue for positive change moves me. I continue to learn from your example of mastery and service. Being willing to stand up in public and speak is courageous. This courage is an example we can all learn from.

Thank you to Jim Halberg and WDRT in Viroqua, Wisconsin, who provided support for our recording and production. We are also grateful to Ursula Ruedenberg of Pacifica Network and the stations that broadcast *Business Matters*.

I have been blessed with teachers, men, and women who helped me see the world differently, challenged me to act with greater integrity, and supported me when I stumbled. These include Dr. Donovan Browne, Mary McDougall, Fernando Flores, Russell Redenbaugh, Will Schutz, Steve St. Clair, and Richard Strozzi Heckler.

As I begin the journey of *Business Matters* again, I am enriched by the writings and programs of Harry Palmer. His example of holding a vision for an enlightened planetary civilization with impeccable integrity and passionate commitment inspires and challenges me to reach deep and give all I have to serving a purpose far greater than myself.

Finally, I express my deepest gratitude to my beloved partner, Elizabeth. Each day, your actions of selfless service warm my heart and show me a way that I wouldn't see otherwise. Your care and unconditional love are beyond anything I have ever experienced and we have only just begun.

Dedication

This book is dedicated to the courageous business leaders who show us the way to a world of mutuality, compassion, and integrity.

How to Read This Book

This book is contextual in nature. Although the actual words won't change, their meaning will every time you read them, as your context will change. Be ready to experience your own AHA moments as you read the insights in this book. They are designed to be standalone actionable messages that will help you think about a challenge you face, a question you are considering, or an opportunity you are exploring differently. As you read this book, please think about the following:

1. When you're reading, write in the underlined area one to three action items that resonate with you.
2. If this content is interesting to you, you can click the link at the beginning of the chapter and listen to the complete interview.
3. Repeat step #1 as often as you are facing challenges or questions about your business or organization, and mark one or more messages that resonate. They will most likely be different than the first time. By the way, this is also a great time to reflect on the messages that resonated with you during your last reading.

Thomas White
Host and Executive Producer

Contents

Introduction	11
Section I Inspirational Leadership	18
Section II Conscious Business: Leading with Purpose and Meaning Dramatically Improves the Bottom Line	30
Section III Willful Blindness—What We Are Unwilling to See and the Cost of What Really Matters	40
Section IV Navigating Change through Greater Awareness and Preparedness for Clear Action	54
Section V How the Business Schools Got It Wrong— Profits at All Costs Isn't Sustainable	66
Section VI Business of Trust: Radically Change Your Potential by Increasing Your Trustworthiness	80
Section VII New Lessons in Innovation from Nature	94
Section VIII How Simplicity Can Change Everything in Our Lives	106
Epilogue	117
Postscript	121
Contributors	125

Introduction

One of my favorite questions that I ask when I'm working with organizations is, "What are the qualities of a great leader?" The answers are surprisingly similar no matter the industry, size, or geography of the company. The top qualities are integrity, reliability, openness, courage, great communication, and having an aspirational vision for the organization's future.

We'll use these qualities to frame the lessons from the eight leaders we feature in this book. These men and women are (or were) masters of their world. They exemplify these qualities and do it in their own unique way. Each of them generously offers their wisdom that, when applied, can be transformational for an organization that adopts it and prepares the members of the organization for change.

In the end, change is the absolute of our world, and it is what we are the least prepared for. Our formal educational world is backward looking. For the most part, we are taught theories and principles that come from the past. We make an assumption that the future will be like the past.

We know little about change and its unpredictable nature. What can we do, then, to prepare for change? The only true preparation is continuous learning. Great leaders have a perpetual state of curiosity—and not the idle curiosity of a dilettante. Great leaders are curious about how things work. They poke and ask questions until they understand the essential nature of an issue.

Now, they may not be experts in the areas of their inquiry. They know enough, though, that when their understanding is mixed with intuition, they can tell when something seems right or not. You see, intuition is the other quality that great leaders cultivate. They know that the best decisions and actions aren't guided only by history. They know there is so much that we don't know and that we have to "trust our gut" to thrive.

The purpose of this book is to stimulate and inspire. If you think things are going pretty well and there isn't much left to learn, please put this book down, as it will be of little use to you. If, on the other hand, you have the curiosity of great leaders and want to explore areas that will give you a deeper awareness of the world, join me for the next eight chapters.

Introduction

This book doesn't contain the answers to your questions. It contains insights and ideas that are there to fuel your quests. If you find that in one or more of the chapters, you're intrigued, then click on the link and listen to our in-depth interview. You will have a first-person experience with that leader and it will leave your life enriched.

This book opens with a conversation with Lance Secretan. Lance is one of the most inspirational men I know. With a background as the head of one of the largest temporary workforce companies, Lance embraced his passion to teach leadership and be a mentor to the top business leaders in the world. He has written over twenty books that disclose new areas of learning and exploration.

Lance isn't your typical leadership teacher. He invites those working with him to the ski slopes of Colorado or the woods of Canada. In these remote locations, Lance, who is over seventy and has the vitality of men half that age, challenges leaders to face their fears and perceived limitations. He encourages them to dig deep into themselves, find their purpose, and ignite a passion to inspire their organizations.

In our interview, Lance simplifies the key elements of inspirational leadership. They are: 1) spark, 2) flame, and 3) torch. Spark is how you inspire yourself. Flame is how you inspire others. Torch is how you inspire the world. What are you doing today to inspire the world?

Being concerned about the qualities of purposeful leadership requires looking beyond the boundaries of the organization and its market. Businesses are not isolated. One of the big changes we are in the midst of is a reformation of our traditional view of capitalism.

Professor Raj Sisodia of Babson College had a vision that the world is different today and that a singular focus on maximizing shareholder value is no longer the most important goal of a company. He put his vision into action and was a founding leader of the conscious capital movement. In our conversation, Raj said, "Businesses operating with conscious capitalism outperform other companies, even financially. When the purpose of the business is for all stakeholders, it's a win-win-win!"

Transformational Leadership

I feel most leaders want to do the right thing. They want to create and grow a working environment that is meaningful. The key to making this a reality starts with the leader becoming clear about their own purpose (which is rarely, "I want to make a lot of money") and then bringing this purpose to the center of the business they lead.

When we talk about courage, we are not limiting it to heroic acts in the face of imminent danger. Courage is called for when we are faced with uncomfortable situations that challenge us to speak up for what we know is right.

Margaret Heffernan, a truly remarkable person, shines a light on one of our least attractive human habits: willful blindness. Willful blindness, in short, is when we know something isn't right and we either do it anyway or ignore it. Often, willful blindness leads to great harm, possibly to a large number of people.

Margaret is an accomplished business leader, author, and BBC producer. She has a voice with clarity about right action. Her three Ted talks have been viewed by over eight-and-a-half million people. Margaret's talks are always uncomfortable because she is willing to challenge our status quo, and she speaks to the values we say we have but sometimes don't live by.

Margaret's book, *Willful Blindness*, was published eight years ago and had such a profound impact that it has just been updated. Our world continues to suffer from the effects of our tendency to bury our heads in the sand. In our interview, Margaret said, "The certainty of our beliefs may hinder our ability to see things more clearly, so we succumb to willful blindness. Would you rather be 'blanket-safe' with your beliefs rather than challenging the norm?" The cost of holding onto the status quo is a world we don't like, and we forget that we are contributing to its creation.

Much of the focus about great leadership is on what we think or feel. What about how we respond due to historic reactions in our body? These reactions influence their effectiveness. This is particularly acute when the leader is unaware of how they react to different situations and how these reactions impact others.

Introduction

We live in times of increasing stress. This stress is aggravated by the pace of business and the demands for response in a world of instant connectivity. Attending to the automatic nature of a leader's reactiveness and how to change it is an area of mastery of Richard Strozzi-Heckler.

Over twenty years ago, Richard was an early pioneer in the evolution of the discipline of Somatics (how we live through our bodies). He has impacted leaders across the spectrum of organizations, from the US Marines to the largest corporations and NGOs. Recently, he has been involved in applying Somatics to the challenges of bringing about clearer understanding and trust in the volatile climate of the politics of the Middle East.

In our conversation with Richard, we explore the impact of change on our bodies and life. Richard says, "Real success happens when leaders are prepared to embrace change in personal practices of clarity and self-awareness. Knowing your center means moving with grace, dignity, and power in times of rapid change and crisis."

Sometimes, I speak with a guest who absolutely surprises me. In the case of Paul Lawrence, I arrived at the interview with some preconceived notions about his views and who he was. I was wrong on almost all counts. Paul Lawrence, at the time of our interview, was a professor emeritus of the Harvard Business School.

Paul was one of the most respected guides of top business leaders from his podium at Harvard, with his many deeply insightful books and his personal advice. Yet, as he reflected on the business climate, he realized that some of the conventional wisdom was just plain wrong.

Starting in the late 1970s, a shift in corporate focus washed over most businesses. The Agency Theory, which says that the primary measurement of success of a CEO and their leadership team is the maximization of shareholder value, radically changed business relationships with customers, suppliers, and employees. Companies, such as IBM, that placed support of the communities where they operated at the top of their corporate values moved to dead last.

Dr. Lawrence said during our discussion that this was plain wrong. He had been studying the writings of Charles Darwin and found this near-sighted approach created a corporate rigidity that would spell disaster if not abated. He also observed, "Business schools taught students to maximize profits and to take advantage of others to be on top and have high salaries. Good leaders, however, are born with a conscience and are not driven only by money." Dr. Lawrence passed away a year after our interview, yet the clarity and vibrancy of his observations are as needed today as they were ten years ago.

One of the simplest truths about business is that the more trust we develop, the greater our true success. A recent study of businesses showed that a decline in trust has a direct connection to a decline in revenues and profits. Yet, businesses continue to fumble in everyday actions to stop a rapid decline. A decline in trust is aggravated by massive breaches in confidence, from data security to fraudulent business practices.

In the past, the types of unscrupulous or negligent business practices that foster broad public distrust were ameliorated by government action. When Enron and MCI were discovered to have committed large-scale deception, the response was broad and swift. Since the Enron convictions, no leader of a major corporation has been prosecuted, even though fraud of massive proportions has been uncovered.

Since legal consequence is no longer a deterrent, corporate governance is. To understand what creates and breaks down trust, David Horsager wrote *The Trust Edge*. From extensive research and study, David offers business leaders a guide on how to assess the level of trust their organizations enjoy and if it's not up to par, what they can do to turn it around

In our conversation with David, he pointed out, "There are eight pillars of trust: 1) clarity, 2) compassion, 3) character, 4) competency, 5) commitment, 6) connection, 7) contribution, and 8) consistency." As our conversation unfolded, we explored each of these qualities and looked at how to weave them into a business culture where trust matters.

In a time of increased innovation from expanding our use of technology, it's good to be reminded that humans are not the only force of innovation in the world. We have created breakthroughs in science and technology. These innovations have forever altered our lives, yet significant challenges persist that impact the safety and security of our existence.

Introduction

Janine Benyus is the founder of the Biomimicry Institute. The Institute fosters the belief that "innovation that seeks sustainable solutions to human challenges can be found by emulating nature's time-tested patterns and strategies." In our conversation, Janine offers new ways to tackle problems, from the simple to the complex, with examples that arise from the observation of nature.

During our interview, Janine said, "The best ideas come from nature—shells, brainpower, and photosynthesis—which we can adapt for human use. They will revolutionize how we invent, heal, and feed the world. Some of our technologies have put us in a cul-de-sac. We're starting to live with the unintended consequences. That's when humility sets in. We ask, 'Where else can I get inspiration?'"

This book ends with a very personal conversation about the art of living well. We spend much of our time working. The average work week in countries such as the US is growing, and in some industries, such as computer technology, working fifty or more hours a week is the norm. At what consequence is a question our guest, Leo Babauta, asked himself.

Caught up in the swirl of financial responsibilities, having less and less time for what was most important and finding himself in a physical condition he found untenable, Leo decided it was time for a change. He radically altered his life to focus on what really mattered. He said as we talked, "We want space to breath and connect to the people who are most important to us. Complexity and hard work are not equivalent to success. Evaluate your commitments and rethink your priorities to reallocate your valuable time to what's most important to you."

His focus is now on simplicity. "Simplicity is an integrated activity. You can't just simplify your work life and forget about your personal life or vice versa. Your journey to simplicity brings all things together for your good." The end result for Leo has been a life where he no longer has debt, travels extensively with his family, and has work that he loves. Everyone can learn from Leo about how to bring harmony into our lives and "have it all."

As we end this journey of discovery, there are simple principles that are revealed. These principles can help us find greater success, not only in terms of financial rewards, although that is possible. The principles offered extend an invitation to live in a way so that all aspects of our lives are rewarding. If our work is purposeful and has meaning, this becomes part of our whole life experience.

One of the unspoken and persistent qualities of those included in this book is that they have different beliefs. They don't accept what others have offered as the only way. They are explorers of the world and their own consciousness. They all are committed to awakening anyone who listens to a world beyond the limitations of our existing thinking. From this expanded view, we can create together a world that is compassionate and that honors the diversity and gifts of those who are part of this shared human experience.

One final note: this book is an appetizer. My intention is to give you a variety of perspectives in the hope that you will find some that not only interest you but inspire you to expand your world. The key points outlined in each chapter give you a view into the conversation I have with each person. For those that you find of interest, I encourage you to click on the interview link and see what you can learn.

Section I

Inspirational Leadership

How we make work meaningful and create true success is through inspiration. Using this inspiration, you can radically alter the success of your organization and build a legacy that is truly valuable to all who are affected by your leadership. Find out the secrets to inspiring yourself, your teams, and the world around you in this section.

To listen to this complete interview, click here:
http://bit.ly/2ZKmrwb

https://www.linkedin.com/in/secretan/

Lance Secretan

Dr. Lance Secretan is the world's top authority on inspirational leadership, a trailblazing teacher, advisor, and expert on corporate culture, whose bestselling books, inspirational talks, and life-changing retreats have touched the hearts and minds of hundreds of thousands of people worldwide. He is the former CEO of a Fortune 100 company, university professor, award-winning columnist, poet, author, and outdoor athlete.

He wrote twenty-one books about leadership, inspiration, corporate culture, and entrepreneurship, as well as an award-winning memoir, *A Love Story*. He is ranked among both "The Top 30 Most Influential Executive Coaches" and "The Top 30 Most Influential Leadership Experts" globally and guides leadership teams to transform their culture into the most inspirational in their industries.

Individuals, entire organizations, cities, and states have experienced remarkable transformations through his unique mentoring, wisdom, and approach.

He has helped six companies to be named to *Fortune's* "Best Companies to Work for in America" list, and eight others are also his clients, and thirty Secretan Center clients are on *Fortune's* "Most Admired Companies" list. Speakers in America ranks him among the Top Five Leadership speakers, and his firm, The Secretan Center, Inc., is ranked number one in the world as an international leadership consulting firm by *Leadership Excellence*.

Section I: Inspirational Leadership

1

Inspiring business leaders do not just increase market shares, meet metrics, and produce profits. They inspire employees to be more successful and customers to do more business with them! #InspirationalLeadership

2

When leaders inspire their subordinates, they unlock potentials that they may not be developing now. #InspirationalLeadership can make a difference.

3

Leadership not only manages but also transforms employees and the workplace to rethink their methods and make them more effective in achieving increased results. #TransformationalLeader

---

4

Human needs that are essential in #Leadership: 1) love and 2) inspiration. We crave to love and be loved, to inspire and be inspired. #InspirationalLeadership

Section I: Inspirational Leadership

5

Inspiring leaders have 1) mastery, 2) chemistry, and 3) delivery. Mastery is doing what they do to the highest standards, chemistry is how they relate with others, and delivery is how they meet others' needs. #InspirationalLeadership

6

For every message, voicemail, meeting, conversation, action, and decision you make, ask yourself if it's inspiring. If it isn't, it's not effective. Make it inspiring! #EffectiveLeadership

_____

_____

_____

7

Regenerating your personal level of inspiration is the key to raising your performance and building meaningful relationships with others. Start attaining your corporate dreams by working on yourself. #InspirationalLeadership

_____

_____

_____

8

Three elements of #InspirationalLeadership:
1) spark, 2) flame, and 3) torch. Spark is how you inspire yourself, flame is how you inspire others,
and torch is how you inspire the world.
http://www.secretan.com/speaking/spark-flame-torch/

___

___

___

9

If you have a deep awareness of who you are and what it takes to inspire yourself, you're already inspiring. #InspirationalLeadership is knowing yourself, how you want to be, and how you want to relate to others. #SelfAwareness

___

___

___

10

When you know who you are and what you want, your influence as a leader emanates, radiates, and inspires!
#InspirationalLeadership

_____

_____

_____

Section I: Inspirational Leadership

11

Great leaders stand out and make a difference because they know the concept of: 1) destiny, 2) character, and 3) calling. They can answer why they are here, who they are, and what they will stand for. #GreatLeaders

---

12

You can't get to the dream of your org with a mere mission statement. A dream is only inspiring once passion connects to a purpose that inspires someone to change the world. #InspirationalLeadership

13

Go beyond your mission and vision statement. Dreams make history and great achievements possible. Are you creating a dream for your org? #MakeHistory

---

14

The ultimate goal of #InspirationalLeadership is to realize breakthroughs and accomplishments that the rest of the world can only hope for.

Section I: Inspirational Leadership

15

Despite all the investments made to change businesses, many leaderships fail because they focus on approaches that don't have a purpose.
It's time to reset! #Focus

_____

_____

_____

16

To be a great leader, you must be equipped with internal resources to inspire other people. Identify:
1) why you are here, 2) how you are going to be; and 3) what you are going to do. #InspirationalLeadership

_____

_____

_____

17

Your legacy is like a torch. It is a beacon of hope and aspirations that you pass from one generation to another. What's your legacy? #Legacy

_____

_____

_____

18

The world is inspired when people are helped to grow. Coach, train, and lead, and you'll share small imprints that will make the future better. What legacy are you leaving behind? #InspirationalLeadership

_____

_____

_____

Section II

Conscious Business: Leading with Purpose and Meaning Dramatically Improves the Bottom Line

Something has happened on the way to success. The rules we have been playing with in regard to corporate cultures have been proven wrong. Research shows that companies with a strong sense of purpose and a clear moral compass actually perform better. Find out why this is so, what you can do as a leader to instill this in your organization, and why so many are holding onto ways that no longer work.

To listen to this complete interview, click here:
http://bit.ly/2LhWKPy

https://www.linkedin.com/in/rajendrasisodia

Raj Sisodia
Raj Sisodia is the F.W. Olin Distinguished Professor of Global Business and Whole Foods Market Research Scholar in Conscious Capitalism at Babson College in Wellesley, Massachusetts. He is also a co-founder and Chairman Emeritus of Conscious Capitalism, Inc.

Raj has written eleven books and over 100 academic articles and is the coauthor of *Conscious Capitalism: Liberating the Heroic Spirit of Business*. His book, *Firms of Endearment: How World Class Companies Profit from Passion and Purpose*, is considered a foundational work in explaining the precepts and performance implications of pursuing a conscious approach to business.

Raj was named one of the "Ten Outstanding Trailblazers of 2010" by Good Business International and one of the "Top 100 Thought Leaders in Trustworthy Business Behavior" by Trust Across America for 2010 and 2011. In 2013 and 2015, Raj was named to the Thinkers 50 list of business and management thinkers from India.

Raj serves on the board of directors of The Container Store and previously served on the board of directors of Mastek Ltd. He is a trustee of Conscious Capitalism Inc.

19

When your company is loved and trusted by your employees and the community, you will have stable, long-term, and mutually profitable relationships with suppliers and other stakeholders. #ConsciousCapitalism

_____

_____

_____

20

Conscious business leadership is the kind that motivates and inspires, as opposed to instilling fear or focusing on people's greed. #ConsciousCapitalism

_____

_____

_____

21

Doing business with #Purpose is when your company makes lives more meaningful—not only for customers but also employees and communities. Now that's extraordinarily special! #PurposeDriven

_____

_____

_____

22

Everybody wants to have a sense of meaning and purpose in life and certainly in their work. Do you have a #PurposeDriven work environment? You can start #Now! #ConsciousBusiness

_____

_____

_____

Section II: Leading with Purpose and Meaning Dramatically Improves the Bottom Line

23

The number-one contributing factor to human happiness is having a good job, which means work that is meaningful and where positive relationships are present. #ConsciousBusiness

_____

_____

_____

24

When work is not about personal self-interest, people actually perform better as a result. People are hungry to embrace this #ConsciousBusiness way of being to see positive change in the workplace. #ConsciousLeadership

_____

_____

_____

25

Be open to take a fresh look at things that you thought you already knew. When you unlearn old ways of thinking and dogmas that aren't working anymore, you discover amazing things. #ConsciousBusiness

26

Companies that operate in a #ConsciousBusiness space take into consideration the #Impact of everything they do for the world. When passion, purpose, and connection are aligned, results are extraordinary!

27

Successful businesses are more about being stakeholder-oriented (with satisfied customers and employees) and less about being shareholder-oriented (simply for profit). #Success

_____

_____

_____

28

Conscious capitalism is a new evolutionary form of consciousness affecting marketing performance and productivity, resulting in doing business more responsibly. #ConsciousBusiness

_____

_____

_____

29

#ConsciousBusiness leadership is about mentoring, motivating, developing, and inspiring people. #ConsciousLeadership

___

___

___

30

When you think about your business's role in society — more than just marketing and making money — you are leading with #Purpose. #ConsciousBusiness

___

___

___

Section II: Leading with Purpose and Meaning Dramatically Improves the Bottom Line

31

Businesses operating with #ConsciousCapitalism outperform other companies, even financially. When the purposes of the business are for all stakeholders, it's a win-win-win-win!

32

#ConsciousCapitalism aims to be the new normal in doing business, where companies have a greater sense of #Purpose — not merely earning money, but reaping benefits of aligning the interests of stakeholders together.

33

Running a business (or working in one) is one of the most noble and beautiful things in the world. It is most fulfilling when done with a sense of mission and higher purpose. #ConsciousLeadership

---

34

Conscious capitalism is an unusual brand of marketing and leadership where world-class companies profit from passion and purpose! #ConsciousBusiness

Section III

Willful Blindness—What We Are Unwilling to See and the Cost of What Really Matters

Willful blindness, what we could and should see but choose not to, has a pervasive effect on us as individuals, as team members or leaders in business, and as members of society. Why do we choose to overlook or ignore things that we know will harm us or others? Why do we blindly follow directives that we know aren't right? Why do we not speak up when we know we don't agree? In the next section, you will learn how to avoid willful blindness and to instead be open to new concepts.

To listen to this complete interview, click here:
http://bit.ly/2LgOKhH

https://www.linkedin.com/in/margaret-heffernan-ab5205

Margaret Heffernan

Dr. Margaret Heffernan is lead faculty for the Forward Institute's Responsible Leadership Program and through Merryck & Co., mentors CEOs and senior executives of major global organizations. She produced programs for the BBC for thirteen years and moved to the US, where she spearheaded multimedia productions for Intuit, The Learning Company, and Standard & Poors. She was chief executive of InfoMation Corporation, ZineZone Corporation, and then iCast Corporation. She has been named one of the "Top 25" by *Streaming Media* magazine and one of the "Top 100 Media Executives" by The *Hollywood Reporter*. Margaret is the author of five books, and her third book, *Willful Blindness: Why We Ignore the Obvious at Our Peril*, was named one of the most important business books of the decade by the *Financial Times*. In 2015, she was awarded the Transmission Prize for *A Bigger Prize: Why Competition Isn't Everything and How We Do Better*. Her TED talks have been seen by over nine million people, and in 2015, TED published *Beyond Measure: The Big Impact of Small Changes*. She holds an honorary doctorate from the University of Bath and writes for the *Financial Times* and the *Huffington Post*.

Section III: Willful Blindness—What We Are Unwilling to See and the Cost of What Really Matters

35

Our inability to see when there are things that we could see but somehow manage not to see is called #WillfulBlindness. It's almost everywhere in the way we lead our lives and make decisions.

_____

_____

_____

36

Sometimes we don't speak up for fear of hurting someone or ourselves. #WillfulBlindness is costly when we choose to overlook or ignore things that we know will harm us or others.

_____

_____

_____

37

By being too comfortable, we're actually in more danger because we're not paying attention to what's happening around us. When we don't pay enough attention, problems arise and grow. #WillfulBlindness

_____

_____

_____

Section III: Willful Blindness—What We Are Unwilling to See and the Cost of What Really Matters

38

Good business leaders engage employees, allow transparency, and communicate openly. How do you create a culture where people feel comfortable putting up their hand and challenging the norm? #ConsciousLeadership

_____

_____

39

Don't merely follow the pack, where you lose sight of your own individuality and your own capacity to respond. Be unique and strong in your convictions. #WillfulBlindness

_____

_____

_____

40

Our brain tends to use our propensity for affinity as a mental shortcut in processing information. It finds familiarity efficient. What mental shortcuts are you too familiar with? #Focus

_____

_____

_____

Section III: Willful Blindness—What We Are Unwilling to See and the Cost of What Really Matters

41

The danger in surrounding ourselves with more things that are comfortable and familiar is that we're deepening our satisfaction but profoundly narrowing our perspectives. #WillfulBlindness

_____

_____

_____

42

If you remain stagnant, you have no growth or increase in life whatsoever. Would you rather keep doing the same things over and over than introduce new ideas to your brain and challenge what you already know? #Success

_____

_____

_____

43

If we stick too closely to the profiles that we already know, we never broaden our outlook or outreach into different areas. #WillfulBlindness

_____

_____

_____

44

Limiting your perspective of the world due to #WillfulBlindness makes it difficult for you to even see or have any understanding of anything or anybody else.

45

#WillfulBlindness can be seen in the polarizing ends of the rich and the poor and in ethnic diversities. Do you only see your side and define the norm to yourself? Or do you also have regard for others?

46

Sometimes bias is neither intentional nor necessarily against a different group. We have a neurological bias in favor of familiarity that we are often not conscious about. #WillfulBlindness

---

47

#WillfulBlindness is taking only whatever is available to you rather than deciding for yourself what you really like, even if it's completely different than the rest. #Integrity

Section III: Willful Blindness—What We Are Unwilling to See and the Cost of What Really Matters

48

Businesses need real scrutiny. Those that go through rigorous study are more successful than those that only trusted familiarity over research. #WillfulBlindness is costly this way.

_____

_____

_____

49

The certainty of our beliefs may hinder our ability to see things more clearly, so we succumb to #WillfulBlindness. Would you rather feel blanket-safe with your beliefs instead of challenging the norm?

_____

_____

_____

50

People are fundamentally obedient to authority, and we don't really like to say "no." Compliance at work is different from merely obeying an order that goes against your morals or values. #WillfulBlindness

51

Many managers and chief executives are not very thoughtful with the orders they set for employees to follow. A successful business does not have a culture of blind obedience. #WillfulBlindness

_____

_____

_____

52

In a competitive environment, if you spend a great deal of time with unethical people, chances are high that you will become unethical. Do not be swallowed by the system with #WillfulBlindness!

_____

_____

_____

53

Ideologies can blind you to data and facts, especially in the context of business. Trends and industry practices change all the time. Be open to new concepts, rather than stay in #WillfulBlindness. #Integrity

_____

_____

_____

Section IV

Navigating Change through Greater Awareness and Preparedness for Clear Action

Change is the only constant of our lives. Yet, we are constantly surprised when change happens. We often resist change until it can't be ignored. Real success comes with preparedness by leaders for change through personal practices of clarity and awareness. Find out these practices, as well as a simple way to be courageous and make a difference.

To listen to this complete interview, click here:
http://bit.ly/2ZGDlvC

https://www.linkedin.com/in/richard-strozzi-heckler-1402962

Richard Strozzi-Heckler

Richard Strozzi-Heckler, PhD, MCC, is an internationally known authority on leadership and mastery. He is a best-selling author and consultant to many of the top corporations in North and South America. His wisdom into leadership has been inspired by his thirty years in business process, linguistics, psychology, biology, aikido, and philosophy. He is known for pioneering the pragmatic application of skillful action to language and purpose in such diverse fields as finance, technology, military, marketing, health, and manufacturing.

Dr. Strozzi-Heckler is a cofounder of Strozzi Institute, Tamalpais Aikido Dojo, and Lomi School, and founder of Two Rock Aikido Dojo. He has taught at the University of Chicago, Sonoma State University, Lone Mountain College, Naropa Institute, and University of Munich. He holds a seventh-degree black belt in aikido, as well as ranks in judo, jujitsu, and capoeira. He has been named one of "The Top 50 Executive Coaches in the Country," listed in *The Art and Practice of Leadership Coaching*.

Dr. Strozzi-Heckler is the author of the nationally acclaimed *In Search of the Warrior Spirit* (chronicling his training of the Green Berets) and has been published in numerous major publications. He is also the editor for the newly released *Being Human at Work: Bringing Somatic Intelligence into Your Professional Life*.

54

We are like protoplasm: diverse and complex. When we go through change, our balance, or homeostasis, is interrupted. To deal with this, we have to contract and protect ourselves. #NavigateChange

55

Change is disquieting. All the parts of your system—mind, emotions, and body—will be a little disorganized. It's time to roll up your sleeves, put your shoulders to the wheel, and steer it lightly! #NavigateChange

56

If you don't notice how upsetting change is, you'll act out of it. Real change happens when you are aware of its process and implications. #MasterChange

57

Awareness means noticing how disquieting and unsettling change can be and making sure to breathe freely, no matter what. #NavigateChange

Section IV: Navigating Change through Greater Awareness and Preparedness for Clear Action

58

It's essential to pay attention to your body, whether you're a four-star general or someone in the mailroom who needs to get messages out to people. When you take care of "you," you're in control. #Attention

59

Create change beyond yourself. Do you know who's on your team? From family, spouse, and any person you lead, look out! Move with them toward awareness, accountability, choice, and freedom! #NavigateChange

60

You are given more choice when you are aware of your body. And that choice comes with both responsibility and freedom. Are you taking care of yourself? #Choice

61

As a leader, you must understand that it isn't easy to control other people. But you can earn trust by starting to manage yourself and paying attention to the life of your body. It all begins with you. #NavigateChange

62

Be with people who can be further in the distance of probability. Begin to design a set of practices and actions that allow you to be stewarded and ferried through the sea of change. #NavigateChange

_____

_____

_____

63

To mediate and move through difficult times in life, it's essential to be grounded in self-generation. This notion of breathing puts you in the center, a place where you can objectively see the world. #Centered

64

When you are centered, you are present in the situation and yourself. You are open to possibilities. You are reminded of your purpose in the world and why you are here. Have you found your balance? #NavigateChange

Section IV: Navigating Change through Greater Awareness and Preparedness for Clear Action

65

The world's rush for materialism and good deals makes it forget humanity. When you are unable to feel your body and self, it will be impossible to feel others.
Are you willing to make a change? #Integrity

_____

_____

_____

66

Change is constant. Your meaningful transition starts with a more enhanced understanding of yourself and the world. Are you ready to rise in the ambiguity of change?
You can make a difference! #NavigateChange

_____

_____

_____

67

As a nation of leaders, you each need to recognize the situation you're in. Whether you like it or not is irrelevant. Discover what needs to change and be an agent for that change! #NavigateChange

_____

_____

_____

68

Many people either don't see change coming or may be in the middle of change, confused. A wake-up call saying that you're under change right now and paying close attention to it is what champs do! #NavigateChange

_____

_____

_____

Section IV: Navigating Change through Greater Awareness and Preparedness for Clear Action

69

Knowing your center means moving with grace, dignity, and power in times of rapid change and crisis. #Centered

70

Three kinds of breaths for a centered well-being:
1) breath of centering the body, 2) breath of centering in your purpose in the world, and 3) breath in centering the mystery of life. #NavigateChange

71

We're in a time when hard work is given too much credit. Do you still look deeply at your values? They can make this world a better place! #Integrity

72

Real success happens when leaders are prepared to embrace change in personal practices of clarity and self-awareness. Are you ready to make a difference? #NavigateChange

Section V

How the Business Schools Got It Wrong—Profits at All Costs Isn't Sustainable

Using vital insights from a lifetime as a Harvard Business School professor and the writings of Charles Darwin, the late Paul Lawrence offered insights into how leaders can adapt and find success. This success should be focused on meeting the four basic concerns that all humans have in all their stakeholders.

To listen to this complete interview, click here:
http://bit.ly/2LfeuuE

Deceased

Paul R. Lawrence

Paul R. Lawrence, a renowned sociologist and a pivotal figure in the intellectual history of Harvard Business School, was one of the world's most influential and prolific scholars in the field of organizational behavior. He was the Business School's Wallace Brett Donham Professor of Organizational Behavior Emeritus. His research was published in twenty-six books and in numerous articles and dealt with the human aspects of management.

Paul Lawrence was an extraordinary person in all facets of his life," said the Harvard Business School dean, Nitin Nohria. "He was a world-renowned scholar who throughout his long career reshaped our understanding of the human side of organizations." His first book, *Organization and Environment: Managing Differentiation and Integration*, was named the best management book of 1967 by the Academy of Management and cited 2,000 times in professional journals. His later works included 2002's *Driven: How Human Nature Shapes Our Choices*, written with Nohria. He published his final book, *Driven to Lead: Good, Bad, and Misguided Leadership* in 2010.

Section V: How the Business Schools Got It Wrong—Profits at All Costs Isn't Sustainable

73

Leadership does not come with a formula. But if we use our brains properly to think, we can come up with an adaptable response to the particular situation we're faced with. #ConsciousLeadership

74

According to Darwin, humans are neither the strongest nor the most intelligent species on earth. But we are the most adaptable to a changing environment. #AdaptableLeadership

75

The genius of what our brain is able to do helps us think our way through finding an answer suitable to the circumstances we're in. #AdaptableLeadership

76

The drive to comprehend is to use the important faculties of imagination, wonder, curiosity, and the power of reasoning. Leaders naturally crave to understand the world around them. #ConsciousLeadership

77

Money is important. But great leaders are motivated more by a desire to have trusted friends rather than just money, and the drive to comprehend how money from business affects the community. #AdaptableLeadership

_____

_____

_____

78

Business schools taught students to maximize profits. They took advantage of others to be on top and have high salaries. Good leaders are born with conscience and are not driven by money alone. #Integrity

---

79

Your business will be more productive when you keep your promises rather than break them. Seek fair exchanges with your stakeholders rather than cheat. #AdaptableLeadership

80

We need to use our creative capacities in doing business with a holistic approach that promotes overall employee satisfaction to ensure productivity and motivation at the highest level. #AdaptableLeadership

81

If you want to be trusted in business and work with stakeholders closely in a truthful way, you will also need to help them fulfill their four drives so that you can truly bond together. #Truth

82

A human's brain is designed to help us in what we need to do if we learn how to use it properly. This is why contextual leadership is a better approach than formulaic leadership. #AdaptableLeadership

Section V: How the Business Schools Got It Wrong—Profits at All Costs Isn't Sustainable

83

In any organization—business or government—the biggest blocker for success is distrust. Train the minds of your leaders to see why trust is important. #Success

_____

_____

_____

84

The fundamental roots of human behavior studied by the father of evolution, Charles Darwin, can help us better understand how humans adapt in business and leadership. #AdaptableLeadership

_____

_____

_____

85

Humans are motivated by four essential drives that act together to shape behavior and can be applied to leadership: 1) to bond with others, 2) to acquire, 3) to defend, and 4) to comprehend. #ConsciousLeadership

---

86

Great leaders are the ones who take into account all four drives from the Renewed Darwinian Theory and constantly learn to adapt to changes in business and life in general. #AdaptableLeadership

---

Section V: How the Business Schools Got It Wrong—Profits at All Costs Isn't Sustainable

87

Man's strength and speed both counterbalance his social qualities, which lead him to give aid to his fellow man and also receive it. Humans are intrinsically driven to think, adapt, and lead. #AdaptableLeadership

_____
_____
_____

88

Friedman economics in business schools used to focus on rewarding only the shareholders at the cost of the other stakeholders. Successful leaders today reward the drives of all stakeholders. #Success

89

The employees, customers, suppliers, community, and investors are your stakeholders. They all deserve your respect and attention in your business. #AdaptableLeadership

90

Human conscience is the most important difference between man and other living species. Man's four drives from the Renewed Darwinian Theory include conscientiousness in business operations. #ConsciousLeadership

_____

_____

_____

91

As a leader, tell the truth rather than lie. Do not mislead your customers by telling them only what they want to hear. #AdaptableLeadership

_____

_____

_____

92

People are misguided by the old agency theory that says you must maximize profit for the shareholders. Balance the four drives from the Renewed Darwinian Theory, and see change happen in your business!

93

When faced with a difficult situation, sit on it for a little while. You'll find four-drive solutions the next morning that you didn't see before. Make the brain work for you. #AdaptableLeadership

---

Section VI

Business of Trust: Radically Change Your Potential by Increasing Your Trustworthiness

What does it mean to be a trustworthy company? A trustworthy leader? A trustworthy individual? David Horsager explains the Trust Edge, how businesses can be hugely impacted by the trust customers have in them, as well as the trust that runs among coworkers. He describes research that has identified the eight pillars of trust, all of which leaders and companies need to have in order to be successful.

To listen to this complete interview, click here:
http://bit.ly/2Lj0znD

https://www.linkedin.com/in/dhorsager

David Horsager

David Horsager, MA, CSP, CPAE, is the CEO of Trust Edge Leadership Institute, national bestselling author of *The Trust Edge*, inventor of the Enterprise Trust Index™, and director of one of the nation's foremost trust studies: The Trust Outlook™.

His work has been featured in prominent publications, such as *Fast Company, Forbes,* and *The Wall Street Journal*. David has advised leaders and delivered life-changing presentations on six continents, with audiences ranging everywhere from FedEx, Toyota, and global governments to the New York Yankees and the Department of Homeland Security.

David and his team at Trust Edge Leadership Institute make it their mission to develop trusted leaders and organizations through inspiring keynotes presentations, executive workshops, benchmarking tools, and annual research. Get free resources and more at www.DavidHorsager.com and www.TrustEdge.com.

Section VI: Business of Trust: Radically Change Your Potential by Increasing Your Trustworthiness

94

The foundation of genuine and long-term success is trust. It is quantifiable, and it brings drastic results to businesses and leaders. #BusinessOfTrust

_____

_____

_____

95

When people believe in you, everything gets done faster in business. Stress, cost, and attrition go down; innovation and creativity go up. #BusinessOfTrust

_____

_____

_____

96

Trust isn't a soft skill. If you believe it is, think about your credit score. It's really just about trust. The more you're trusted by a lender, the less you pay. #BusinessOfTrust

_____

_____

_____

97

There are eight pillars of trust for leaders:
1) clarity, 2) compassion, 3) character, 4) competency,
5) commitment, 6) connection, 7) contribution, and
8) consistency. #BusinessOfTrust

_____

_____

_____

98

Leaders create a culture of trust in an organization. It starts by stating a compelling and clear vision that subordinates can trust. What's the vision of your company? #BusinessOfTrust

---

99

It's natural to put faith in leaders who are kind and compassionate. If you want your people to trust you, be a leader who thinks beyond one's self. #Compassion #BusinessOfTrust

---

100

Trustworthy leaders will always choose what's right over what's easy. They do exactly what they say they'll do. Are you willing to take challenges for the benefit of your org? #Character #BusinessOfTrust

_____

_____

_____

101

People have confidence in leaders who can stay fresh, relevant, and capable, no matter what the cost is. #Competency #BusinessOfTrust

102

Leadership produces long-term relationships and revenues when everyone is committed. #Commitment happens when a leader shows exactly what it is as an example. #BusinessOfTrust

103

Trust makes any business, organization, or relationship. The more trust, the less everything costs and the higher the loyalty of everyone involved. #BusinessOfTrust

_____

_____

_____

104

A trusted leader is followed and emulated by salespeople, and a trusted salesperson creates a credible brand that many customers pay more for and buy. Trust is the currency of business! #BusinessOfTrust

105

A #BusinessOfTrust leads to greater morale, innovation, and productivity. Is your business centered around trust?

106

Trust has an interesting dichotomy. People trust those who are transparent yet confidential. Know when to be private and stick to your word! #BusinessOfTrust

_____

_____

_____

107

How can you repair broken trust? Rebuild trust by making and keeping commitments. Everyone makes mistakes. It's about owning up to them. #BusinessOfTrust

108

Trust isn't earned overnight. It requires time, effort, diligence, and character. Strive for it and make a difference! #BusinessOfTrust

109

The fastest way to increase influence, impact, and business results is leading with trust. Push the priorities of your org, increase engagement, and earn the trust of those you lead! #BusinessOfTrust

---

110

Trust accelerates sales cycles. High-performing sales teams bring consistent sales with focus and clarity! #BusinessOfTrust

111

The greatest organizations of all time are trusted! They have a trusted brand where people pay more, come back, and tell others! Increase your profitability by building a #BusinessOfTrust.

_____

_____

_____

Section VII

New Lessons in Innovation from Nature

We think our minds are the only place that innovation comes from. Actually, innovation has been happening in nature long before we humans showed up. Learn how to think about innovation beyond your limitations. Learn the lessons of nature for the design of success and sustainability.

To listen to this complete interview, click here:
http://bit.ly/2ZL1n8u

https://www.linkedin.com/in/janine-benyus-a5626

Janine Benyus

Janine Benyus is a cofounder of Biomimicry 3.8, a B-Corp social enterprise providing biomimicry consulting services. She is a biologist, innovation consultant, and author of six books, including *Biomimicry: Innovation Inspired by Nature*. Since that book's 1997 release, Janine's work as a global thought leader has evolved the practice of biomimicry from a meme to a movement, inspiring clients and innovators around the world to learn from the genius of nature.

In 2006, Janine cofounded The Biomimicry Institute, a nonprofit institute that was created to embed biomimicry in formal education and in informal spaces such as museums and nature centers. Over eleven thousand members are now part of the Biomimicry Global Network and they practice, teach, and spread biomimicry. In 2008, the Institute launched AskNature.org, an award-winning bio-inspiration site for inventors. Janine has received numerous awards, including the 2016 Feinstone Environmental Award, the Rachel Carson Environmental Ethics Award, the Lud Browman Award for Science Writing in Society, and the Barrows and Heinz Distinguished Lectureships. In 2012, she received the Smithsonian Institution's Cooper-Hewitt National Design Mind Award, given in recognition of a visionary who has had a profound impact on design theory, practice, or public awareness

Section VII: New Lessons in Innovation from Nature

112

Nature has already fixed myriad societal problems with animals, plants, and microorganisms as experienced engineers. Have you been putting nature's lessons into practice when it comes to innovation? #InnovationFromNature

_____
_____
_____

113

Real transformation in business happens when we treat our ecosystem as our mentor. This is what the growing field of biomimicry is all about! #InnovationFromNature

114

We were used to just looking at how other humans and cultures succeed. Now the next big step is seeing how the natural world is an enormous database of not only knowledge but also wisdom. #InnovationFromNature

115

We're up against the same limits that other organisms have already been living with. Science gives us the answers about how things work, and technologies enable us to emulate that greatness. #InnovationFromNature

116

Our human society has the capacity to sustain the world if we can only get inspiration from the natural organisms all around us. #InnovationFromNature

117

The aesthetic of the world is changing. How can we do something with materials that are more common and renewable? It's about time we switch our mindset. Beauty is what works for people and the planet. #InnovationFromNature

Section VII: New Lessons in Innovation from Nature

118

Nature provides a model that humans can imitate for designs and processes. #InnovationFromNature

_____

_____

_____

119

Judge the rightness of human innovations by using ecological standards as the measure. #InnovationFromNature

120

Technologies are meant to enhance a system, not deplete it. When they don't, we begin to doubt our technological prowess. It's the same as saying that we must take cues from an octopus instead of an engineer. That's humility. #InnovationFromNature

Section VII: New Lessons in Innovation from Nature

121

The best ideas in innovation come from nature—shells, brainpower, and photosynthesis—which we can adapt for human use. They will revolutionize how we invent, heal, and feed the world. #InnovationFromNature

122

Nature has its time-tested strategies and patterns. Use them to innovate and find sustainable solutions to human problems. #InnovationFromNature

123

Some of our technological approaches have put us into a cul-de-sac, and we're starting to live with the unintended consequences. That's when humility sets in. Where else can we get inspiration? Nature! #InnovationFromNature

Section VII: New Lessons in Innovation from Nature

124

Things don't get created in a vacuum in nature. They're part of an intricate web of relationships, and humans tend to forget the impact of all the things they touch until they go back to nature to awaken them to consequences. #InnovationFromNature

125

Humans should mimic nature in three broad areas: 1) form, 2) process, and 3) ecosystem level. This is where the real bang for the buck is! #InnovationFromNature

126

The ecosystem has a characteristic that we could apply to companies: resilience. A resilient ecosystem is one that can get disturbed and then come back to its original form. #InnovationFromNature

_____

_____
_____

Section VIII

How Simplicity Can Change Everything in Our Lives

Most of us feel that our lives are far too complicated. This complexity leads to overwhelm and burnout. The end result is unhappiness in our work and personal lives. In this chapter, we will find the value of simplicity in creating a meaningful life.

To listen to this complete interview, click here:
http://bit.ly/2LfzIho

https://www.linkedin.com/in/leo-babauta-4248477b

Leo Babauta

Leo Babauta is a simplicity blogger and author. He created Zen Habits, a Top 25 blog with a million readers. He's also a best-selling author, a husband, father of six children, and a vegan. In 2010, he moved from Guam to San Francisco, where he leads a simple life.

He started Zen Habits to chronicle and share what he's learned while changing a number of habits, including:

- Quit smoking (on Nov. 18, 2005).
- Became a runner.
- Ran several marathons and a 50-mile ultramarathon.
- Began waking early.
- Became organized and productive.
- Began eating healthier
- Became a vegan.
- Eliminated his debt.
- Simplified his life.
- Lost weight (about 70 pounds).
- Wrote several best-selling books and ebooks.
- Started a successful blog on simplicity.
- Created a leading blog on minimalism.

Section VIII: How Simplicity Can Change Everything in Our Lives

127

Ask other people to hold you accountable. It helps to stay committed on your journey of #Simplicity. If you do things privately and no one notices, it's easy not to pursue the changes you wish to see in your life.

128

Make public commitments. This will motivate you to stick to the small steps you're taking to see changes in your life. #Simplicity

129

We want space to breathe and to connect with people who are important to us. We don't always have that space because of things we have unconsciously built up in our lives. #Simplicity

---

130

Most people want to do many changes all at once, and that doesn't work. #Simplicity is about starting small and doing it in little steps.

Section VIII: How Simplicity Can Change Everything in Our Lives

131

We go through our lives just accumulating complexity through technology and demands from our jobs and personal lives. We want #Simplicity because we want #Peace in our lives.

_____

_____

_____

132

Cut back on activities that keep you busy and see what happens. Experiment. Don't allow fear to stop you from changing things in your life, a little at a time. #Simplicity

_____

_____

_____

133

If you do one change at a time, one small step at a time, it's much easier and longer lasting. #Simplicity

134

All over the world, there is an outpouring of interest for people to live simpler lives. Take a step back, and evaluate your choices to make necessary changes that will benefit your life. #Simplicity

Section VIII: How Simplicity Can Change Everything in Our Lives

135

Complexity and hard work are not equivalent to success. Evaluate your commitments, and rethink your priorities to reallocate your valuable time to what's really important to you. #Simplicity

136

When your life feels upside down, check your priorities. These can be the biggest indicators of why things aren't working out. What are the areas (as well as who) in your life do you give most of your time to? #Simplicity

137

When you make one small change in your life and gradually make more small changes along the way, it becomes your new normal. #Simplicity is sustainability.

_____

_____

_____

Section VIII: How Simplicity Can Change Everything in Our Lives

138

Getting out of debt can be a wake-up call to #Simplify. You become stress free and you will have peace of mind when you don't have that extra weight of paying off your debt on your shoulder! #Simplicity

139

#Simplicity is an integrated activity; you can't just simplify your work life and forget about your personal life or vice versa. Your journey to #Simplicity pieces all things together for your good.

140

When eating habits change, your attitude toward moving your body also changes. From a sedentary lifestyle, you become a more alert and productive person. #Simplicity ripples its effect across your mind, body, and soul.

_____
_____
_____

Epilogue

One of the most surprising aspects of this book was the answer to one question I posed to most of our broadcast guests. I asked, "When you look out ten years from now, what do you see that is different?" While the answers were diverse, there was a common thread. They were hopeful that human behavior would become kinder and that leaders would see the folly of the status quo and would make substantial changes in how they did business.

Ten years have passed since some of the interviews, and I realize how little is different. In fact, from most perspectives, things have gotten more extreme. Polarization of the political discourse has intensified. The gap between the compensation of the top leadership of organizations and the average worker wage has increased. Trust of public and private institutions is at an all-time low.

Particularly in the United States, business practices haven't shown a substantial change, with one exception. That is the increasing number of small and medium-sized businesses that are operating with a different set of beliefs. Rather than maximizing shareholder value above all else, they know it's vital to act with integrity, serve the good of all constituencies, act with respect for the environment, and support their local communities.

There is other good news as well. In a small number of large organizations, workers are changing their perspective about what they can demand of the companies they work for. They feel that the actions of the organizations to whom they devote their most productive resources, their time, and their talent must more closely reflect what matters to them.

In the 2019 Edelman Trust Barometer (an annual global study of the trust of institutions and the media), a surge in employee expectations was noted. Both current and prospective employees expected their employer to share their concern for societal issues. That included strong support of broad corporate initiatives such as The Unilever Sustainable Living Plan.

Last year, over twenty thousand Google employees from fifty offices protested the company's handling of high-level executives accused of sexual harassment. Microsoft employees presented a petition protesting their company's involvement

Epilogue

in facilitating immigrant detention. Employee activism is not widespread, and there has been strong resistance from company leaders.

We are at a tipping point. If we put our attention on these changes and through our collective efforts, give them the support required to take deeper root, the pendulum will swing swiftly toward greater care for all. If, on the other hand, we are spectators who talk about what needs changing and don't engage in change with our committed action, the pendulum can easily swing back to greater isolation of ourselves from the consequences of our actions. Making these types of changes has four elements: inspiration, clarity, commitment, and deliberate action.

With the relaunch of *Heart of Business*, we focus on conversations that inspire. Inspiration that arises from the stories of companies and their leaders and teams who are "on the front lines" of creating a new norm. We also will bring stories of what I call "workplace activists." These are people who have the courage to take a stand for what matters to them, even at the risk of the disfavor of the company that employs them.

Sometimes, we feel like we are playing a game of "whack-a-mole" in fostering change. Every time we make a shift to do something that we feel is better, something we didn't anticipate or thought was handled is in our face. Why do so many of us experience this? It is because we are focusing our attention on the symptoms of our challenges rather than the cause.

What we are trying to do is change our experiences. We don't want to experience low sales or customer problems or deliver our newest products late. You know the litany of things that show up as challenges. Now, the key is to understand what is causing these experiences. It might surprise you to know that these challenges all come from our beliefs.

We are a maze of beliefs about everything, from what we like and don't like to what we believe is possible or not. We are unaware of most of these beliefs, and we are adding to our library of beliefs every day. We even have beliefs that are conflicting—beliefs like, "I know we can do it," and, "I'm not sure we can do it this time." In fact, things that we believed in the past that supported success may no longer be viable.

As we expand our support of a different way of doing business, we will explore this phenomenon. We will help our listener identify beliefs that are helping businesses experience success and beliefs that are getting in the way of what businesses envision.

It's easy to say that you are for something that you feel is noble. The challenge is to live in the commitment of doing what's required to experience what you espouse. Sometimes, it requires uncomfortable or courageous actions. Other times, it's a matter of being deliberate in your choices to make sure your decision supports what matters to you. We will offer conversations with people who share their experiences of their personal journey of doing what they feel is right, so our listeners find support and a feeling of not being alone.

Choosing what's in integrity must be coupled by deliberate actions that meet the expectations of everyone involved. This is hard work. The world is always changing, so it's vital to have a simple, consistent process that assures you do what you say. The payoff is trust. It's time we reverse the trend of distrust to encourage all we come into contact with that they, too, can act in this way.

To help stir the pot, so to speak, we will publish new books similar to this one that will include our most recent *Heart of Business* interviews. If the change of the status quo in business is important to you, consider right now what you can do. How can you be an agent of change in your workplace and community?

Postscript

When you listen to a radio program or a podcast, you may think the program is easy to produce. After all, in the case of interview-oriented programs, how much work can there be? Two or three people sit down and talk, and that's that.

When I first started *Business Matters* ten years ago, I pretty much thought that too. But when I started the program, the work really began. It involved finding the best people to provide our audience with insights and inspiration, getting them interested in taking time out to talk with us, and then coming up with a schedule that worked for everyone. After that, there was the preparation for the interview. Many great interviewers put in many days of preparation for a single interview. That's how you ask perfect questions that bring out the best during an interview.

After the interview, there is the production part. Everyone doesn't speak in perfect sentences. They sometimes meander when they talk. While that may be how they speak, it won't engage an audience. That is where the editing of the interview begins. One must listen to each interview over and over, smooth out the rough edges, and nip and tuck where needed. The editor will also listen for the best short segment, and that often becomes part of the program lead-in.

Then comes the process of putting everything together. More needs to be recorded in order to tell the story of the episode, introduce the guest, add commentary, and take the program in and out of breaks. *Business Matters* wasn't a podcast. It was broadcast program that we produced in a fifty-nine-minute format each week. We had to make sure that we hit the mark perfectly for the time format—and our editors did it!

Even after all of that, the work isn't done. There are conversations with radio stations, talking to program directors and general managers, encouraging them to place a program on their regular schedule that is already full. Their concerns must be listened to, and one must do what one can to meet any special needs they have.

All of this takes a team. A team that loves what they do? Each week, the team makes the program sound different, and over time, they make it sound better. We were blessed to have a great team from the beginning to the end of the our first run.

Postscript

Below, you can see some pictures of "how the sausage was made." I have also included, along with my picture and information, the same for the co-hosts of *Business Matters*. Through their engagement, they brought the best out of me and our guests and gave our listeners a great experience every time.

What makes *Business Matters* work so well is that we have two hosts for each program. Each person brings a unique point of view and that broadens the scope of the questions we ask and the exploration we undertake. My only regret is not taking full advantage of all that they offered. That is part of my own learning process and is part of the mix in the future.

Prudence Tippins

Prudence Tippins is a couples and family therapist living in the Pacific Northwest. She is experienced as a teacher, a teacher trainer, a retreat center owner/facilitator, an intergroup dialogue facilitator, and a writer. She has always been interested in what can make life better for humans and their terrestrial companions. *Business Matters* was a notable part of that quest.

Kelly Helmuth

Kelly is the cofounder of Bestest, a new mobile app that lets you poll the public and vote right from your phone. Since it launched in September 2018, the app has logged four million votes and has amassed 43,000 users. Before Bestest, Kelly spent five years in business innovation, facilitating the cross-pollination of ideas between startups and multinational corporations. She is the ghostwriter of *Unlock Your Inner Entrepreneur* (The Editing Company, 2012) and a graduate of Georgetown University. She started her first company at age twenty-one and grew it to seven figures in sales.

Business Matters had amazing editors and producers. They smoothed out the "ah-hhs" and "umms" and made sure that the essence of the program was there and that everything else was cut away. That team came from a broad variety of backgrounds, including professional producers, volunteers in community radio, and musicians. Each person brought a commitment to having the program be at its best each week.

Postscript

Here is a photo of a typical session in our studios with producers Bill Motlong and Charlie Knower and co-hosts Prudence Tippins and Thomas White.

Contributors

Name of Contributor	
Lance Secretan https://www.linkedin.com/in/secretan/	Section I
Raj Sisodia https://www.linkedin.com/in/rajendrasisodia	Section II
Margaret Heffernan https://www.linkedin.com/in/margaret-heffernan-ab5205	Section III
Richard Heckler https://www.linkedin.com/in/richard-strozzi-heckler-1402962	Section IV
Paul R. Lawrence Deceased	Section V
David Horsager https://www.linkedin.com/in/dhorsager	Section VI
Janine Benyus https://www.linkedin.com/in/janine-benyus-a5626	Section VII
Leo Babauta https://www.linkedin.com/in/leo-babauta-4248477b	Section VIII

Business Matters appreciates the support of its sponsors. These sponsors' messages are on the following pages.

Leadership Solutions from
Eddie Turner, The Leadership Excelerator®

Organizations who want to accelerate the development of emerging leaders call Eddie Turner, The Leadership Excelerator®. He is an in-demand expert who has worked for several of the world's "most admired companies" such as Deloitte, GE and Accenture. Eddie works with leaders to Accelerate Performance and Drive Impact!® through the power of facilitation, the art and science of coaching and professional speaking.

Eddie is a C-Suite Network Advisor and a national media commentator who holds international certifications as a trainer, facilitator and coach—including being one of around 15% of speakers in the world to earn the Certified Speaking Professional™ (CSP®) credential from the National Speakers Association. He is also a published writer of content for Forbes.com and other national publications. Eddie is the international best-selling author of 140 Simple Messages to Guide Emerging Leaders and the host of the Keep Leading!™ podcast, designated as New & Noteworthy by Apple Podcasts.

- ★ Leadership Development
- ★ Executive Coaching
- ★ Leadership Coaching
- ★ Workshop Facilitation
- ★ Board Retreats
- ★ Learning Delivery
- ★ Professional Speaking
- ★ Master of Ceremonies
- ★ Moderator

eddieturnerllc.com +1 (312) 287-9800

Grow Your Business Using Masterminds

Quickly build ongoing revenue streams with a scalable one-to-many offer you build once and sell repeatedly.

Discover how the Mastermind process has become the ultimate tool for business leaders. By leveraging existing experience and intellectual property you increase profit and authority.

We help you create:
- A high profit program
- A competitive advantage
- An additional revenue stream

Web: www.eccountability.io
Email: info@eccountability.io

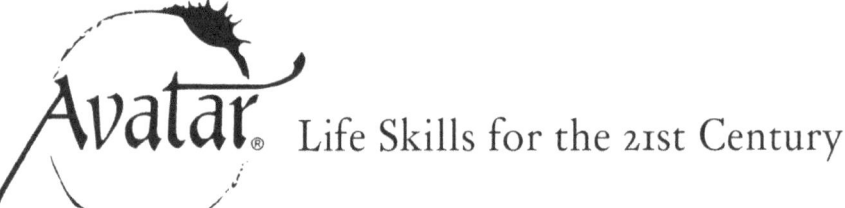

Avatar® Life Skills for the 21st Century

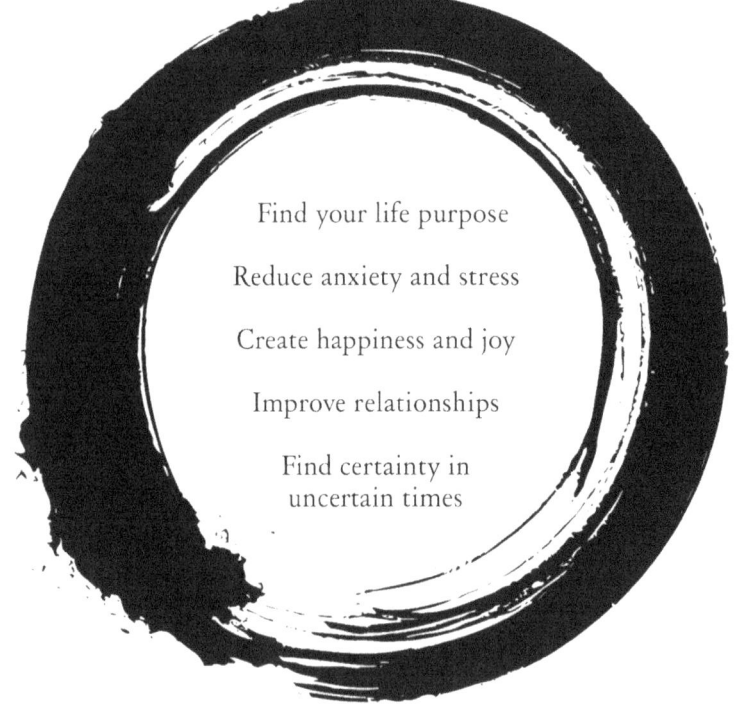

Find your life purpose

Reduce anxiety and stress

Create happiness and joy

Improve relationships

Find certainty in uncertain times

Changing lives for 30+ years

Available in 22+ languages

100,000+ successful students in more than 153 countries

For more information please visit http://bit.ly/2LmHDEm
or contact Beth White: bethwhite@livingwithavatar.com / 408.384.4240

> Are you a busy, successful professional that **wants more credibility** and would want that credibility through a book, but don't have the time?

Imagine four months from today

being an Amazon bestselling author where we have written, published, distributed, and drove the Amazon bestseller campaign and you have spent **between five to ten hours.**

For more info, please go to
https://AHAthat.com/Author
and schedule a 30-minute strategy call to focus on your situation by going to
http://aha.pub/focused.

The publisher, THiNKaha, has created the AHAthat platform for you to share the content from this book socially. Click here to share:
https://aha.pub/BusinessMatters

CPSIA information can be obtained
at www.ICGtesting.com
Printed in the USA
BVHW061237150720
583703BV00004B/23